TO:

....

FROM:

....

DATE:

....

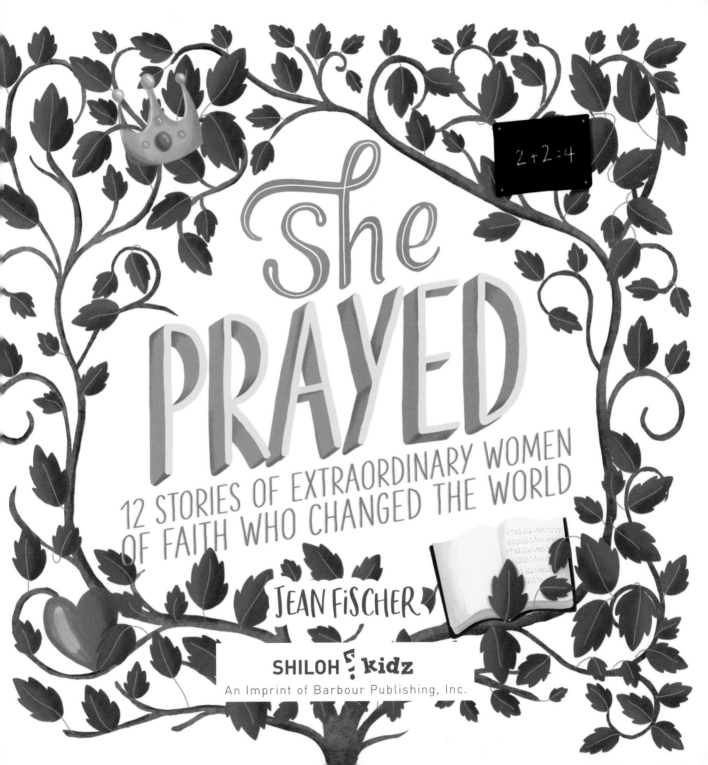

She PRAYED

12 STORIES OF EXTRAORDINARY WOMEN OF FAITH WHO CHANGED THE WORLD

JEAN FISCHER

SHILOH kidz

An Imprint of Barbour Publishing, Inc.

Published by Shiloh Kidz, an imprint of Barbour Publishing Inc., 1810 Barbour Drive, Uhrichsville, Ohio 44683, www.shilohkidz.com

Our mission is to inspire the world with the life-changing message of the Bible.

Member of the
Evangelical Christian
Publishers Association

Printed in China.
000296   0620   HA

THESE EXTRAORDINARY WOMEN OF FAITH CHANGED THE WORLD!

DEBORAH
(Judges 4–5)

A THANK-YOU PRAYER TO GOD

Deborah was the only woman judge in the Bible. God spoke to Deborah, and she told others what He said.

She told a man named Barak, "An enemy general and his army are coming after God's people, and God wants them stopped." Barak asked Deborah to go with him to fight the army. Together they led God's army, the Israelites, to win.

Deborah sang a thank-you prayer to God. She thanked Him for allowing the Israelites to win the battle with their enemy.

Have you ever sung a prayer to God? Try it. He would love to hear your song.

"O give thanks to the Lord. Call upon His name.
Let the people know what He has done. Sing to Him.
Sing praises to Him. Tell of all His great works."
1 CHRONICLES 16:8–9

FAYE EDGERTON
(1889–1968)

A PRAYER FOR HELP

God created every language on earth. He understands everything people say. But with all those different languages, people don't always understand each other.

Faye Edgerton, an American missionary, wanted everyone to have a Bible they could understand. The Navajo people didn't have a Bible in their language. So Faye began the work of translating the New Testament into Navajo. She asked God for help learning the words. The Navajo language was very hard to learn. But Faye did it! She gave the Native American tribe their own Bible.

Maybe you would like to learn another language, so you can tell others about Jesus too!

There are many languages in the world.
All of them have meaning to the people who understand them.
1 CORINTHIANS 14:10

Faye Edgerton

ESTHER
(Esther 1–10)

A PRAYER TO SAVE HER PEOPLE

Queen Esther had a big secret: Her husband, the king, didn't know she was Jewish.

An evil man named Haman lied about the Jews, and then the king ordered all Jewish people to be killed. Esther's cousin, Mordecai, heard the lies, and he told Esther. To save her people, Esther had to tell the king she was Jewish.

Esther prayed and asked God for help.

When Esther told the king her secret, he let all the Jewish people live. He rewarded Mordecai for being good, and he punished Haman for lying.

Esther knew to ask God for help. He is ready to help you too!

Do not worry. Learn to pray about everything.
Give thanks to God as you ask Him for what you need.
PHILIPPIANS 4:6

Esther

ELIZABETH FRY
(1780–1845)

A PRAYER TO HELP OTHERS

Elizabeth Fry spent her whole life helping the poor. She saw terrible conditions in England's prisons, and she became like an angel to the women there. She prayed for them and taught them about God. Elizabeth asked the queen and other leaders for help making the prisons better. Her prison mission grew and was well known all over Europe. Many people were helped by Elizabeth's kindness. She never gave up. She prayed hard, stood up to those who were against her, and she made sure things got done.

How can you be like Elizabeth and help others? Ask God to show you what you can do.

The Spirit of the Lord God is on me, because the Lord
has chosen me to bring good news to poor people.
He has sent me to heal those with a sad heart.

ISAIAH 61:1

Elizabeth Fry

HANNAH
(1 Samuel 1; 2:1–21)

AN UNSELFISH PRAYER

Hannah prayed asking God to give her a baby. She promised God if He gave her a son, she would allow the temple priests to raise him. He would grow up learning to serve his heavenly Father. God gave Hannah what she wanted, and Hannah kept her promise. She allowed the priests to raise her little boy.

Baby Samuel grew up to be a great man, a priest, a judge, and a prophet. He is remembered even today for his wisdom.

Hannah was willing to give God the one she loved most, her baby. Could you be that unselfish?

"You must give your whole heart to him and
hold out your hands to him for help."
JOB 11:13 NCV

Hannah

ANNE HUTCHINSON
(1591–1643)

A COURAGEOUS PRAYER

Anne Hutchinson was one of the first American women to speak up about her faith. She lived in the Massachusetts Bay Colony when women were not allowed to speak up or lead others in prayer. But Anne, who thought for herself, decided she wasn't going to keep quiet! She held prayer meetings in her home and was arrested for breaking the law. Still, she stood up for what she believed was right. She bravely prayed in public and shared her faith with others.

Anne's actions helped give women the courage to continue speaking up and fighting for what they believe. Ask God to help you be courageous in your faith too!

Open your mouth for those who cannot speak,
and for the rights of those who are left without help.
PROVERBS 31:8

Anne Hutchinson

ESTHER IBANGA
(1961–)

A PRAYER FOR PEACE

In Nigeria, where Esther Ibanga is a pastor, Christians and Muslims don't get along. But Esther wanted to create a good change. So she reached out to Muslim women, hoping that together they might find a solution and maybe even friendship. She and her new friends began the Women Without Walls Initiative. Their goal is to reach Nigeria's children and help them get along, so someday there might be peace.

Esther was raised in a family that prayed. She prays every day for peace among Christians, Muslims, and people all over the world.

Do you pray for peace in the world? Think of three things you can do to help people get along.

"Do not hurt someone who has hurt you.
Do not keep on hating the sons of your people,
but love your neighbor as yourself."
LEVITICUS 19:18

Esther Ibanga

MAHALIA JACKSON
(1911–1972)

A PRAYER of PROMISE

Whenever Mahalia Jackson sang, she prayed and promised God she would use her voice to honor Him. And she kept her promise.

Many people heard Mahalia sing, and she became famous. She recorded albums, sang for President John F. Kennedy, and, in the 1960s, was invited by Dr. Martin Luther King Jr. to sing at the March on Washington for civil rights. Using her voice to honor God led Mahalia to become an international star. Today she is remembered as one of the greatest gospel singers ever.

Have you made a promise to God? If so, ask Him to help you keep it.

My lips will shout for joy when I sing praise to you—
I whom you have delivered.
PSALM 71:23 NIV

Mahalia Jackson

HELEN KELLER
(1880–1968)

A POWERFUL PRAYER

Helen Keller became blind and deaf as a little girl. It seemed impossible that she would be able to learn anything. But then a teacher, Anne Sullivan, helped Helen learn and live in the world around her.

God was always with Helen. She prayed and felt His power and love. With God's and Anne's help, Helen learned to read, write, and speak. Helen asked God for power to do more, and she accomplished great things. Helen gave speeches, traveled the world, met famous people, and received many awards.

Maybe there is something you want to do even better. Remember Helen's story. Ask God for power to do more.

I can do all things because Christ gives me the strength.
PHILIPPIANS 4:13

Helen Keller

LOTTIE MOON
(1840–1912)

A HEARTFELT PRAYER

Lottie Moon caused trouble at school. Her friends prayed and asked God to help Lottie behave. God answered their prayers. Lottie lay awake one night, thinking about her behavior. She knew she needed Jesus, so she prayed and asked Him into her heart.

Lottie's love for Jesus led her to China and missionary work there. She made lots of friends. Because of Lottie, many people accepted Jesus as their Savior.

None of what Lottie accomplished might have happened if her friends hadn't prayed. Do you know kids who cause trouble? Pray for them. You never know: God might have plans for them to do His work.

"But I tell you, love those who hate you. (Respect and give thanks for those who say bad things to you. Do good to those who hate you.) Pray for those who do bad things to you and who make it hard for you."
MATTHEW 5:44

Lottie Moon

PANDITA RAMABAI
(1858–1922)

A PRAYER THAT LEADS TO GOOD THINGS

Pandita Ramabai grew up in India. Her family didn't know Jesus. They worshipped false gods.

One day, Pandita saw Christians helping others and sharing Jesus' love. This got her attention! Pandita wanted to know their Jesus, so she prayed and asked Him into her heart. She read the Bible and learned from Jesus how to help others.

Pandita set up schools, orphanages, and women's shelters. She taught others in India to live as Christians honoring the one, true God.

Do you believe there is only one true God? Pandita learned that trusting in Him leads to everything good.

"Have no gods other than Me."
EXODUS 20:3

Pandita Ramabai

PHILLIS WHEATLEY
(1753–1784)

A PRAYER OF TRUST

Phillis Wheatley was the first African American and the first US slave to publish a book of poetry. Many of her poems were about God.

As a slave, Phillis worked for the Wheatley family. They taught Phillis to read and write. She was smart and learned about many different things. Phillis especially loved writing! The Wheatley family freed Phillis from their ownership. As a free woman, she continued to write and sell her work.

The Wheatleys were Christians, and Phillis had learned from them about Jesus and prayer. She faced many problems in her life, but Phillis got through them all by praying and trusting God as her Helper.

Do you talk to God often? Do you trust Him as your Helper?

I have called to You, O God, for You will answer me.
Listen to me and hear my words.

PSALM 17:6

Phillis Wheatley

MORE GREAT BOOKS FOR COURAGEOUS GIRLS LIKE YOU!

100 Extraordinary Stories for Courageous Girls

Girls are world-changers! And this deeply inspiring storybook proves it! This collection of 100 extraordinary stories of women of faith—from the Bible, history, and today—will empower you to know and understand how women have made a difference in the world and how much smaller our faith (and the biblical record) would be without them.
Hardback / 978-1-68322-748-9 / $16.99

Cards of Kindness for Courageous Girls:
Shareable Devotions and Inspiration

You will delight in spreading kindness and inspiration wherever you go with these shareable *Cards of Kindness*! Each perforated page features a just-right-sized devotional reading plus a positive life message that will both uplift and inspire your young heart.
Paperback / 978-1-64352-164-0 / $7.99

The Bible for Courageous Girls

Part of the exciting Courageous Girls series, this Bible provides complete Old and New Testament text in the easy-reading New Life™ Version, plus insert pages featuring full-color illustrations of bold, brave women such as Abigail, Deborah, Esther, Mary Magdalene, and Mary, mother of Jesus.
DiCarta / 978-1-64352-069-8 / $24.99

With your parent's permission check out CourageousGirls.com, where you'll discover additional positive, faith-building activities and resources!

SHILOH ! kidz
An Imprint of Barbour Publishing, Inc.